Secret Treasures

Secret Treasures
for
WISDOM

by Kimberly Perry

"Kimberly Perry's book is a gem. It is an artistic treasure, made even more beautiful because Holy Scripture is woven into prayer and personal reflection. WHAT A JOY!"

Rev. Theodore K. Parker, OSC
Catholic Priest, St. Cecilia
Detroit, Michigan

Unless otherwise indicated, all Scripture quotations are taken from the Amplified Translation of the Bible; The Amplified Bible, Old Testament copyright 1965, 1987 by The Zondervan Corporation. The New Amplified Bible New Testament, copyright 1958, 1987 by the Lockman Foundation.

Paintings & Collage Art by Author and Artist, Kimberly Perry
Graphic and Page Design by Simpson Communications, 248.443.9880

Secret Treasures Series
Secret Treasures for Wisdom

ISBN 0-9718440-0-3
Copyright 2002 by Kimberly Perry

Celebrations of the Spirit Publishing
27350 Southfield Road, PMB #133
Lathrup Village, MI 48076

To order copies of Secret Treasures for Wisdom see order
form in the back or order online at:
www.secrettreasurebooks.com
248.443.9633

What does it all mean?

The symbols on the cover of this book, as well as throughout various pages of Secret Treasures for Wisdom, embrace very special, heartfelt meanings to me. Keep these meanings in mind as you journey through these Secret Treasures for Wisdom, and let God speak to your heart, unlocking the Secret Treasures of His Word to you. Write your thoughts on the journal pages for easy reference at future dates.

In His Love, Kimberly

 This symbol represents God's infinite love.

This symbol stands for the Trinity: God the Father, God the Son, and God the Holy Spirit.

 This symbol speaks to our journey through this life in God.

This symbol relates to the Word of God, which is the water of life.

Contents

God's words are life, healing, & health.

May this book be a blessing to you, your family, and your friends. The Secret Treasures in this book will be discovered by reading, meditating, and applying these life-changing Scriptures to your life. Just as our physical bodies need food, our spirits need daily nourishment as well. God's words are life to those who find them and healing and health to all their flesh. I pray that God's words will bless you.

Kimberly Perry

Introduction

Secret Treasures

The Secret Treasure Series are books filled with meditations and prayers. The series consist of topics that cover a wide variety of subjects that are sure to touch your life in a special way. They make great gifts for family and friends.

Share the gift of life!

Celebrate!

My inspiration for my artwork comes from God, the greatest Artist in the world.

GOD

created every color in this world,
every shape, twist, and twirl.
Let us celebrate these wonderful beauties;
we owe it to the Creator as our duty.

☀ *Kimberly Perry* ☀

My inspiration for writing the Secret Treasures Series is based on Psalm 1:1-3. God tells us if we habitually meditate on His Scriptures day and night, everything we do shall prosper. The Bible is filled with secret treasures that will richly bless your soul, spirit, and life.

In order to increase your wisdom, follow this instruction:

☀   Each day ask yourself, "How can I apply this to my life?"

Start today. Whatever the Holy Scriptures tell you, if you obey, you will discover the treasures God has waiting for you.

THE GRASS WILL
WITHER
THE FLOWERS WILL
FADE
But THE WORD OF GOD
WILL STAND FOREVER
Isaiah 40:8

Kimmy 1895

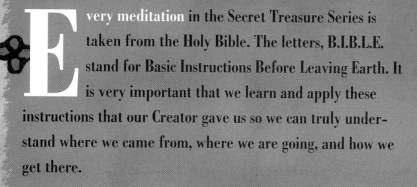

Every meditation in the Secret Treasure Series is taken from the Holy Bible. The letters, B.I.B.L.E. stand for Basic Instructions Before Leaving Earth. It is very important that we learn and apply these instructions that our Creator gave us so we can truly understand where we came from, where we are going, and how we get there.

Also, God wants us to *enjoy* the journey. Please take your time with each meditation, because they are much more than just words on paper. They are sharp, alive, empowering, life-changing, and life-enhancing!

Meditation of the Scriptures should be a daily, spiritual exercise. This daily meditation will change your life from mediocrity to excellence.

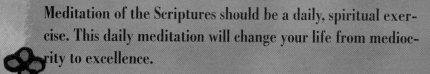

My writing and my art are my ways to fight Satan and all the lies that he uses to deceive people. My hands and fingers are fighting a daily, spiritual warfare. The war is against spirits and principalities fighting over your soul and your faith. We have to fight the good fight of faith and never give up hope in God's promises to us.

My goal is to prevent Satan from stealing your joy, peace, courage, and faith. I would like to teach people to cling to God and the Bible. Believe every word in it, and let God speak to you, teach you, love you, and save you!

Blessed is the Lord

My rock and my strength:

He teaches my hands to war

And my fingers to fight.

Psalm 144:1

17

Personal Testimony

I thank God for taking me out of darkness and placing me into His light. Before I became a born-again Christian, I made my decisions in life based on what I read in fashion magazines, what my friends said (which was always something different from each of them), what I saw on television, or what I just felt like doing. You never really know if you're making the right decision when you live life like this.

Finally, I discovered the Holy Bible, which is the ultimate light and truth for the world. My confusion was finally **gone**! I knew what God, my Creator, wanted me to do. A light turned on in my life. God's words will give wisdom to whomever seeks it. The Scriptures chosen in this book will increase your wisdom and change your life.

My confusion was finally gone!

I have learned your statues

Afflictions

Meditation One

It is good for me that I have been **afflicted** in order that I have learned your statutes.

Psalm 119:71

Many times situations occur in our lives that make us uncomfortable. We ask ourselves, "Why did this happen to me?" God's Word tells us that it is through our afflictions and trials in life that we learn our greatest lessons.

Why Me God?

26

Dear God,

Thank you for teaching me lessons in life. I know that when I have problems and am weak and vulnerable, that is when I grow the most spiritually. When I don't have the answers is when I can turn to You and You will teach me, show me, and strengthen me. Lord, thank you for showing me your power, love, mercy, and grace. I thank you for the gift of life. I know this is preparation for my eternal life.

Amen.

Self
Expressions
for
Healing

What **hard times** have you gone through?
What **lessons** did you learn from them?

anger

A

[pru◉dent]

Cautious, Discreet

Anger

A fool's anger and wrath are quickly and openly known, but a prudent person ignores an insult.

Proverbs 12:16

34

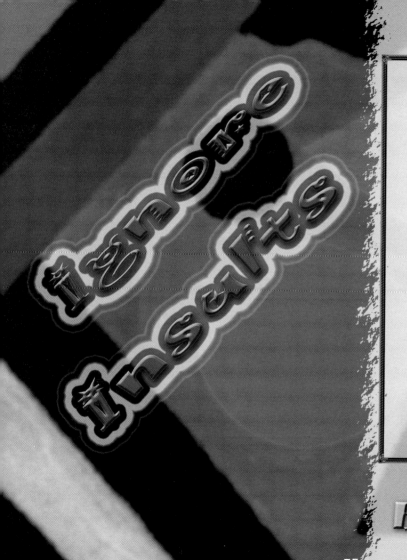

Ignore Insults

When someone **insults** you or is very unkind to you, having a quick temper, wrath, anger and hatred toward that person hurts you more than it hurts the other person. Ignoring an **insult** makes you the wiser person.

Be Wise

Thank you Lord for words of Wisdom

Prayer

Dear God,

Thank you for these words of wisdom, Lord. You know it is so easy to lose patience with people, especially if someone insults us. We want to return the insult. However, starting today, I will be the wiser person.

I know I can ignore insults from people, because I know who I am. And I know You created me, you love me, and I'm yours! I know you forgive me when I make mistakes, and I know You still love me anyway. I love you too.

Amen.

Give Thanks

List 10 Things You're Thankful for TODAY

Love

Meditation Three

If I can speak in the tongues of many men
and even angels but have not love,
then I am only a noisy gong or a clanging cymbal.

I Corinthians 13:1

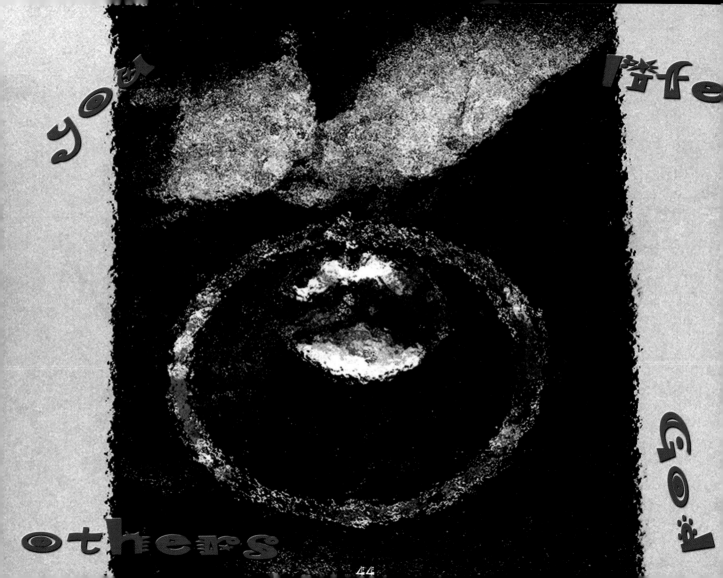

You can be a very wise and educated person. You may have many gifts and talents. But if you cannot love yourself, your life, and others, then your conversation and words are like a clanging cymbal.

Love yourself, your life, & others

Love Never Fails

Prayer

Dear God,

Help me to truly understand what it means to love, to be loved, and to give love. Lord, I know in I Corinthians 13:4-8 you tell us how to love. You tell us to be patient and kind, long suffering, not conceited, touchy or fretful. Lord, starting today, I promise I will try my best for You. I will try to express love to others in everything I say, and I know love never fails!

Amen.

How do you express love to your loved ones? How can you improve?

GOd, help me to love.

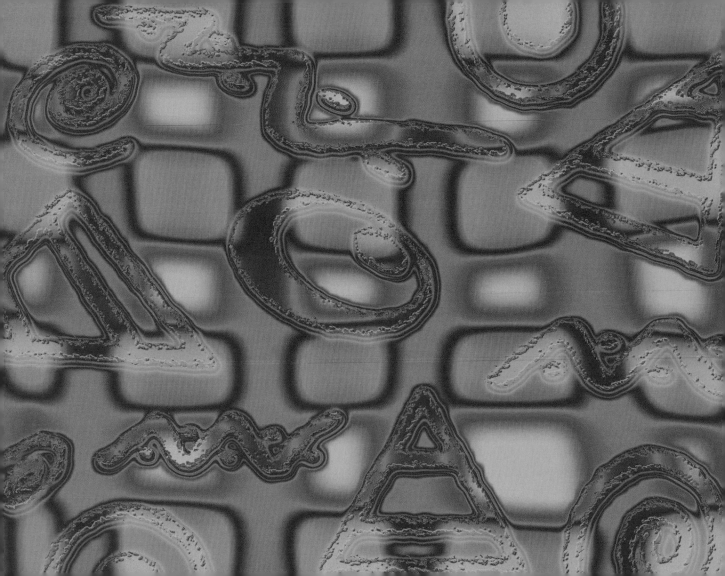

family

forgive

Forgiveness

Meditation Four

For if you forgive others their
trespasses, your heavenly Father will also
forgive you. But if you forgive not men their trespasses, neither will your father forgive your trespasses.

Matthew 6:14 -15

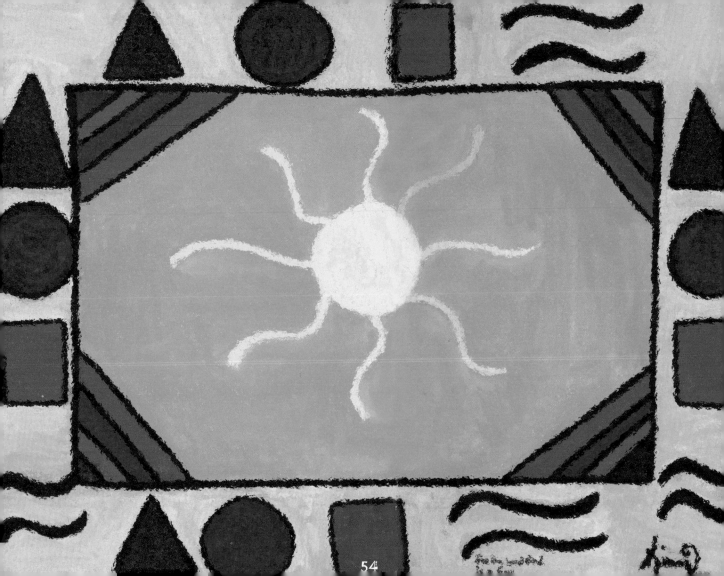

If you ask God to forgive you when you sin, He will! However, He wants us to have the same **mercy** and **grace** toward others, just as He has for us. Every human being on earth will make mistakes. **forgive them!** This is the key to true freedom and peace.

Love your enemies

Prayer

Dear God,

In Luke 6:35-38, your Word tells us to love our enemies, to be merciful and sympathetic. You tell us to judge not and we will not be judged. For the measure we deal out will be measured back to us. Lord, I realize now, when I don't forgive my enemies, I am being disobedient to You. Therefore, right now, I forgive all the people (name them) who have hurt me in the past. I now realize that it is not my job to judge and to condemn them. You are the Lord of the Heavens, and I release them to you. I am now free from all anger and heaviness that comes from unforgiveness. I strive to love and have compassion for all mankind as You do. Thank you Lord for revealing this treasure to me, in understanding how important forgiveness really is. Amen.

Show

Mercy

What are your emotions at this moment?

How do you feel most of the time, and why do you feel this way?

Forgive

Meditation Five

The Holy Bible **shall not depart** from you. You shall meditate on it day and night, that you may observe and do according to all that is written in it. For then you shall make your way prosperous and then you shall **deal wisely** and have good success.

Joshua 1:8

Do you want to be **successful** in every area of your life? Well, God gave us a manual to read and follow to achieve this.
The **Holy Bible** will give you wisdom and answer every question you have about life.

Prayer

Dear God,

Please forgive me for being so stubborn. I know that your specific instruction to me is to read the Bible day and night and then I shall deal wisely. Please forgive me for being disobedient and rebellious. Starting today, I surrender my all to You. I have tried things my way, and I was not fulfilled.

Now I am ready to totally follow You, and I know I will be blessed. When I become lazy please strengthen me by the Holy Spirit, and when I am blinded to my own desires, please open my eyes so that I may truly see.

Amen.

Plan a daily schedule that you will be committed to. Set aside a special time every day to nurture your soul by praying, studying God's teachings and meditating.

Prosperity

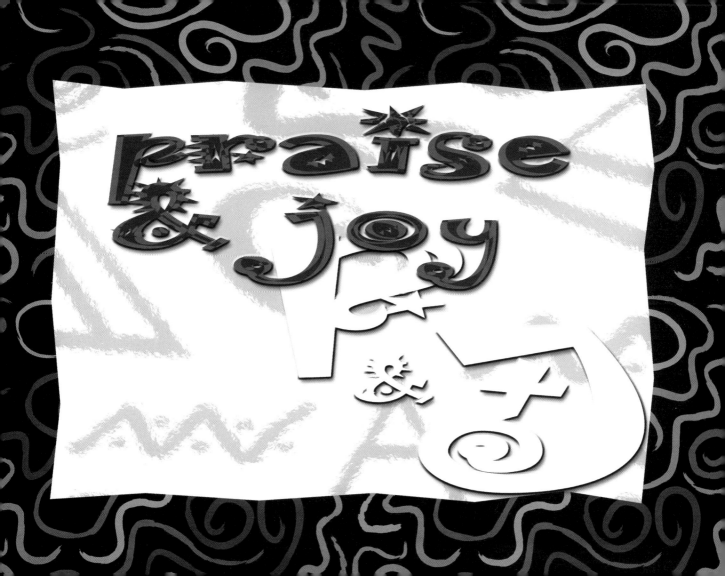

Meditation Six

Let me live so that I can praise You,
and let Your decrees help me.

Psalm 119:175

Praise & Joy

give Him praise!

Do you ever wonder
why you were born? Why were
you put on this earth?

The Holy Bible tells us we were given life
to *glorify* God our Creator. He wants us
to love Him and praise Him daily. True
joy comes from *praising* God!

Prayer

Dear God,

What a wonderful and beautiful revelation! "Let me live so I can praise You." Lord, I humble myself right now to worship You, to glorify You, to magnify You, and to exalt You. You are worthy. You are mighty, and You are powerful. You are loving and forgiving; you are truth. You are the Light. You are my joy. You are my everything! Every day on this earth is a gift from God. Every day that I am given this gift I will praise You, love You and thank You.

Amen.

praise the Lord!

praise the Lord!

Write down things in your life for which you are thankful. Then raise your hands and praise the Lord!

Health & Healing

Meditation Seven

A happy heart is a good medicine, and a cheerful mind works healing, but a broken spirit dries up the bones.

Proverbs 17:22

Broken in Spirit?

You are healed!

Do you know someone who is sick and tired all the time? They go to the doctor and the doctor can't find anything wrong with them. This is usually a person who has a broken spirit.

They need love, encouragement, counseling, and prayer.

I will have a happy heart!

Prayer

Dear God,

In Philippians 4:8, You tell us, "If there is anything worthy of praise, fix your mind on it, take account of and concentrate on it. Lord, starting right now, I choose to be obedient to your Word. I will concentrate my thoughts on the positive things in my life. When negative thoughts creep in, I will capture them, refute them, and dissolve them with the Word of God. I will have a happy heart, because I choose to concentrate on lovely, wonderful, healing, and happy thoughts.

Amen.

Are you happy?

Explain why or why not.

What steps can you take in your life to increase your joy to another level?

Submission to God

Meditation Eight

Haughtiness comes before disaster,
but humility before honor.

Proverbs 18:12

Courage, Strength, & Wisdom

Courage, Strength, & Wisdom

It takes more courage, strength, and wisdom to remain humble. All honor and glory should be given to God for every good thing on earth.

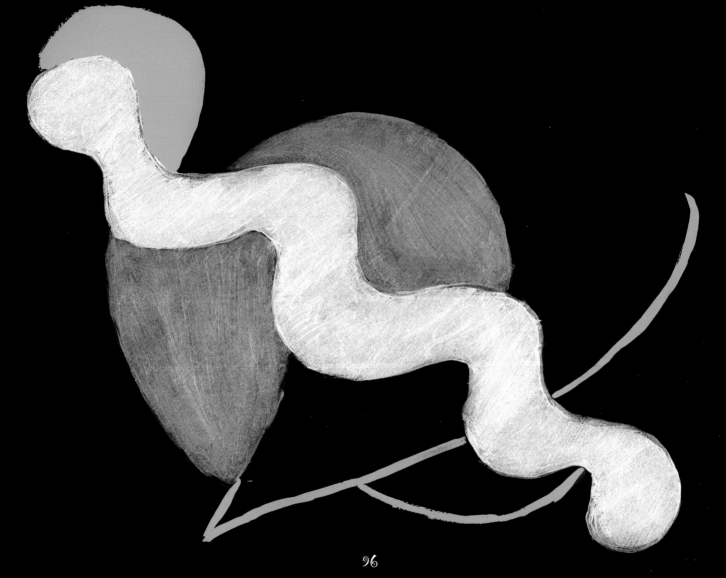

Dear God,

Please forgive me for being prideful and arrogant. Father, you give grace to the humble. Therefore, starting right now I humble myself and submit to Your words of wisdom. I refuse to let my flesh, my emotions and my own personal satisfactions rule me. I understand now that only You have the ultimate wisdom that I need to be happy in life.

My emotions and thoughts change daily, However, Your Word is constant and always right. I know I can trust your guidance and Your wonderful promises provided for me. Father, starting at this very moment, I humble myself to Your authority. I will follow Your guidance and I will always acknowledge You and praise You for being Lord of my life.

Amen.

Prayer

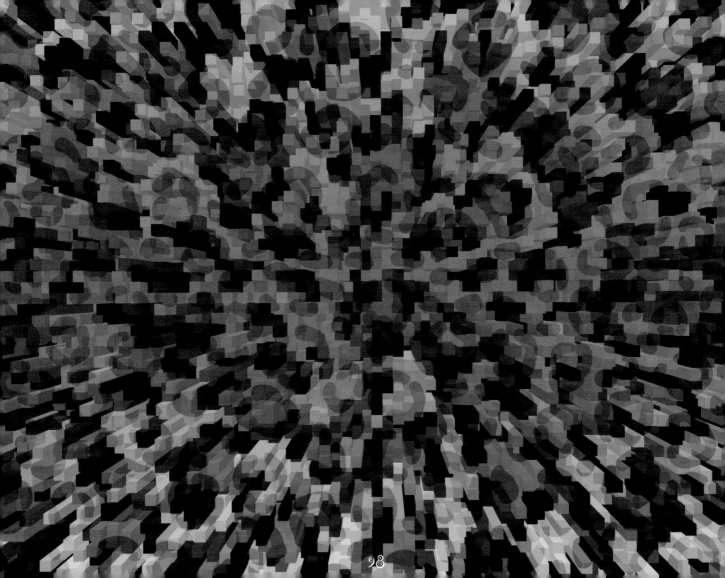

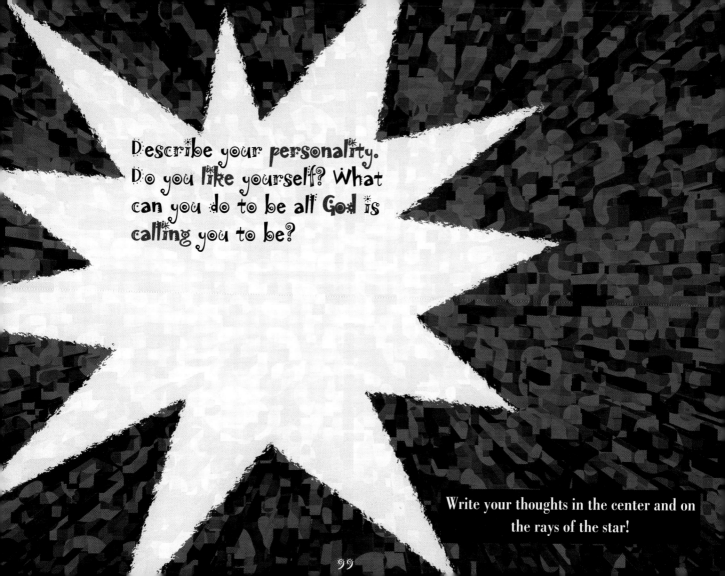

Describe your personality. Do you like yourself? What can you do to be all God is calling you to be?

Write your thoughts in the center and on the rays of the star!

Strength & Power

Meditation Nine

**I have strength for all things
in Christ Who empowers me.**

Philippians 4:13

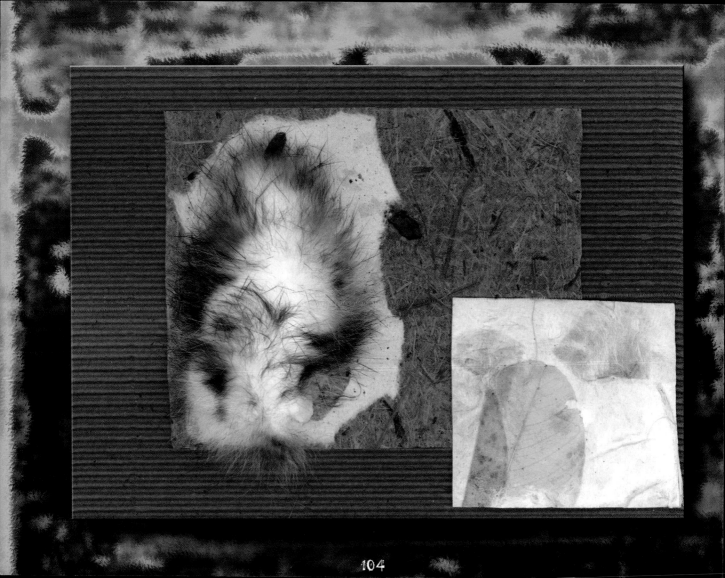

 **G**od will never give us more than we can handle. If we lean on God, He will give us strength and *power*.

Lean on God

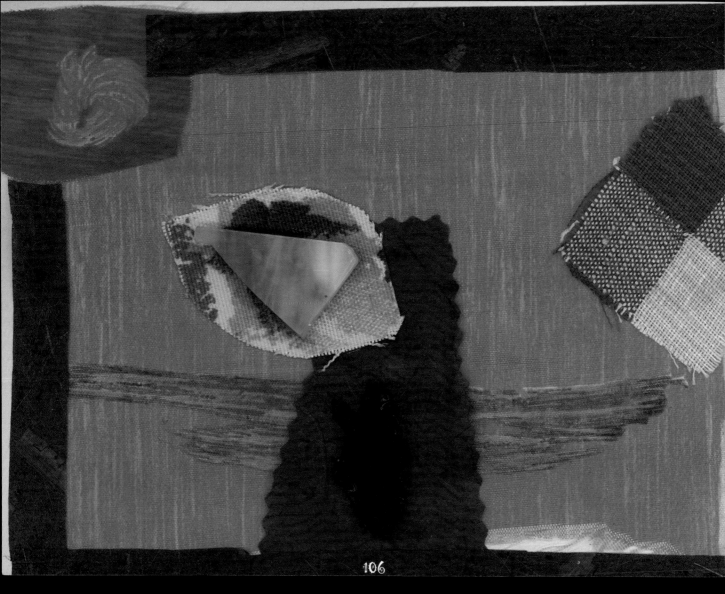

Prayer

Dear God,

Sometimes it is so hard to handle all the responsibilities that I have. There are many days when I don't know how I will make it through, But, Father, I trust in you. And your Word tells me that I have the strength to accomplish all things when I allow my Father to empower me. Therefore, at this very moment, I surrender all to You, Lord. I cast all my worries and cares on You. Your promises from the Holy Bible, Your infinite love and never-ending mercy will empower me daily. Starting today, every day I will meditate on Your Holy Scriptures. As a result, I will get stronger spiritually and physically every day of the rest of my life. Thank you Father.

Amen.

Empowered

Empowered

Empowered

Empowered

Empowered

Empowered

Empowered

Empowered

Empowered

Empowered

Empowered

What steps do you personally take, on a daily basis, to strengthen yourself physically, mentally and spiritually?

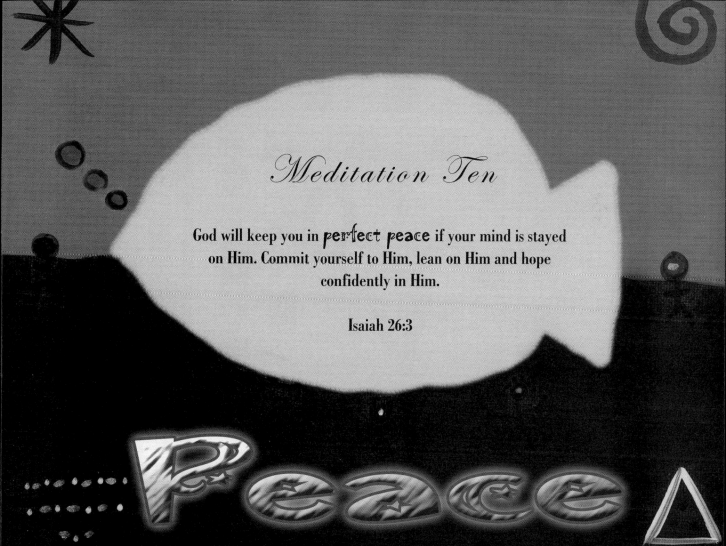

Meditation Ten

God will keep you in **perfect peace** if your mind is stayed on Him. Commit yourself to Him, lean on Him and hope confidently in Him.

Isaiah 26:3

I f you are **searching** to have more peace in your life, God is the answer. Study His words and promises to you. Spend time in **prayer** daily, and throughout your day meditate on how you may apply **God's Word** to every situation in life!

Need Peace?

Thank you
God
for peace!

Prayer

Dear God,

I pray for *peace* in my life, in my mind, in my soul, and in my spirit. Not as the world gives, but as You give. I pray for a peace that transcends all understanding. People will be in wonder and awe, because I will have such a strong, *undisturbed peace*. No person or circumstance will be able to steal this away from me. Nothing shall offend me or make me stumble, because starting right now, my mind will always be on You and Your words of wisdom. From this day forward, *I will lean on You*, commit myself to You, and will always have hope because of You. I thank You Lord for Your gift of peace.

Amen.

What steps can you take to have
a deeper level of peace
in all areas of your life?

Live Forever

If you want to live forever and ever, you can! The choice is yours. Your physical body will give out one day, but your spirit can live on throughout eternity. There's a wonderful place called Heaven that awaits you when you leave Earth. John 3:16 of the Holy Bible tells us, "For God so greatly loved the world that He gave His only begotten Son, that whoever believes in Him shall not perish, but have everlasting life."

All God wants us to do is believe in Him! Trust Him and make Him the Lord of the your life. Acknowledge the heavenly Father and receive His Son Jesus Christ as your Savior and you will not perish. You can live forever!

If you want to grow spiritually and truly understand more about God and His Son, Jesus Christ, I encourage you to read the Bible, meditate on His Holy Scriptures, pray to Him, and go to church to fellowship with other believers. A whole new world of joy, peace, health, and prosperity await you! Start today with the prayer on the next page, and know that you will live forever.

Prayer for Eternal Life

Dear God, my heavenly Father,

I believe in You. I confess You and Your Son,
Jesus Christ, as my Savior.

I love you for creating me and giving me the gift of life. I
thank you for forgiving me of all my mistakes and
allowing me to return to You in Heaven when
I am done with my assignments on Earth.

Amen. I believe.

Celebrations of the Spirit Publishing Company
Secret Treasures Series
Order Form

I am excited about Secret Treasures for Wisdom. I would like to order more copies for friends and family!

Name: _____

Address: _____

City: _____

State: _____ Zip: _____

Daytime Phone: _____

Evening Phone: _____

E-mail Address: _____

Item#	Qty.	Item Name	Price Ea.	Total
ST01		Secret Treasures for Wisdom	19.95	
WP01		Secret Treasures for Wisdom Poster	5.00	
		Subtotal:		
		CA residents please add appropriate sales tax		
		Postage & Handling		
		TOTAL		

Method of Payment

❏ Check ❏ Visa

❏ Money Order ❏ MasterCard

When ordering by charge card, please complete the following:

Card#_____

Expiration
Date_____

Signature_____

Make checks & money orders payable to
Celebrations of the Spirit Publishing

Postage & Handling

Standard: $3.00 for 1st item; $1.00 each additional item.

Second Day: $9.00 for the 1st item: $2.00 each additional item.

Next Day: $14.00 for the 1st item: $3.00 each additional item.

Ordering Information

To order copies of Secret Treasures for Wisdom, please contact:

Celebrations of the Spirit Publishing
27350 Southfield Road, PMB #133
Lathrup Village, Michigan 48076
www.secrettreasurebooks.com
248.443.9633

Kimberly is available for speaking engagements. You may contact her at: 248.443.9633.

Or you may e-mail her at: Kperry1234@aol.com.

Speaking Engagements

Kimberly Perry